Books by Lazaris

LAZARIS

Working with Your Shadow:
An Imperative on the Spiritual Path

... A Workbook for the Spiritual Journey Home

NPN Publishing, Inc.
P. O. Box 691867, Orlando, FL 32869

LAZARIS

Working with Your Shadow: An Imperative on the Spiritual Path
A Workbook for the Spiritual Journey Home

© 1995 NPN Publishing, Inc.
P. O. Box 691867, Orlando, FL 32869
1-800/678-2356

1st Printing 1995, 2nd Printing 1998

Photographs by Michaell North

ISBN 1-55638-289-8

Dedication

This book is dedicated to Peny,
the one we came to touch,
the one who truly touches us.
We love you.

— Lazaris

THE LAZARIS MAILING LIST

To be placed on Lazaris' mailing list, please call or write Concept: Synergy, 1-800/678-2356, P. O. Box 691867, Orlando, FL 32869.

LAZARIS ...

For as long as there is Light ...

"We are here to remind you that pain and fear are not the only methods of growth, that you can more elegantly grow through joy and love ... that you do create your own reality ... that there is a God/Goddess/All That Is who loves you, who knows your name ... and that you love — you love 'good enough.'

"For as long as there is Light ... and the Light is forever ... we shall love you."

— Lazaris

Since 1974 Lazaris has channeled through Jach Pursel, his only channel, offering his friendship and love and generating a remarkable body of tools, techniques, processes, and pathways for our Spiritual Journey Home to God/Goddess/All That Is.

He has touched thousands in his extraordinary workshops, and tens of thousands more with the books, video tapes, and audio tapes that many have said are the finest tools of metaphysics and spirituality available.

We invite you to explore the Love, the Light, the Joy, and the Wonder which is the Spark of Love known as Lazaris.

A Note about Lazaris' Use of Language

Throughout this book Lazaris refers to himself as "we." Ever since he began communicating with us in 1974, he has done that. Lazaris says that each of us has many selves, but that right now we are experiencing them one at a time, and thus we refer to ourselves as "I." Lazaris has many selves as well — many selves in many dimensions — but experiences them all simultaneously and therefore refers to himself as "we." It is not the use of the "parental we" or the "editorial we," but rather a reflection of Lazaris' experience of his own reality.

Also, often you will find that Lazaris will use a plural pronoun or modifier in a place you might expect to find a singular one. This is done to avoid using the generic masculine pronouns which tend to make women feel as if they are not included in what is being said. To make certain they do know they are included, Lazaris often uses plural pronouns which, though against the rules, are better aligned with what is true.

Finally, much of the material in this book is taken from the Evening with Lazaris audio tape *Working with Your Shadow: An Imperative on the Spiritual Path.* We have retained in the written form indications of audience response which do much to pass along the resonance of safety, warmth, humor, and love which Lazaris created in talking about this topic.

Contents

Working with Your Shadow:
An Imperative on the Spiritual Path

Resources

The following Lazaris tapes are helpful in working with some of the issues in Chapter 1 or offer further exploration of related areas:

> *Giving Voice to Your Soul: Greater Spiritual Depth*
> *Reclaiming Your Lost Depth of Soul: Awakening Your Spirit*
> *The Magic of Receiving: A New Dimension of Success*

1

The Magic of the Shadow Work

*The Shadow holds the secrets of change, change
that can affect you on a cellular, on a human
level — change that can affect your very DNA.*

— Lazaris

Whether your metaphysics is but weeks or months
old or whether it is years or decades old, each of you
is always beginning and is always continuing to work
with the Shadow Self. Such work is never done.

*When you can
make peace with
your Shadow
Self, the tangled
briar of obsta-
cles and limita-
tions can begin
to die, and you
can be free.*

And in our time together, we are going to take that
never-done Shadow Work to new dimensions and to
new depths. It is a pleasure and a joy and an honor ...
yes, an honor ... to be a part of your Shadow Work, to
participate in what you are about.

It is the Shadow and the Shadow Work that so
often holds the clues to your resistance — the resistance that is far deeper than your current linear intellect, logic, and reason can understand.

So often you've asked *Why do I resist receiving?*

You've asked, and you've answered, sometimes very cogently and very powerfully. But the answers were never quite enough, because there are reasons that you resist that go far beyond your current intellect and far beyond your linear logic and reason.

It is the Shadow that holds the clues. The Shadow also holds the secrets of change, change that can affect you on a cellular, on a human level — change that can affect your very DNA.

The Shadow also holds the treasures, the treasures that allow you not only to be a person who knows how to receive, but also which allow you to be a person whose nature, whose instinct, is to receive.

With a foundation of understanding and awareness, you also can come to know the immensity and the intensity of your own Shadow, of *your* Shadow, and to begin to harness, to direct, and to use that Shadow to create a reality more magical than before, to create a reality filled with more wondrous successes than before.

When you really make peace with your Shadow, your life, your reality, can be filled to overflowing with all kinds of magic, all kinds of miracles. You know that when you make peace, when you really make peace, the very process of creating can become so rich and so ripe — sometimes richer and riper than the creation itself. Surely the creation itself does produce grand treasures of achievement, accomplishment, and success. But the process of creating can offer and produce grand treasures of realness, of a real self, of your spirituality.

When you can make peace with your Shadow Self, the tangled briar of obstacles and limitations can begin to die, and you can be free. You can be free to transform yourself and the world around you. You can be free to begin to transcend your fears and shames, failures and pain.

And beyond the peace with your Shadow, you can begin to make peace with your Self. And then truly your life can be filled with all kinds of magic, all kinds of miracles, rich and ripe — your life can be dripping with magic and miracles. And your life can be filled and overflowing with rewarding friendships and intimate relationships, with meaningful work and with fulfilling successes. You can discover the uniqueness of your own worth and your own value. You can discover the uniqueness of your strengths, of your power, and of your talents. Oh yes, and indeed you can come to know your Soul, you can come to know your Spirit, and your relationship with God/Goddess/All That Is can be alive and vibrant with life and embracing love. And your spirituality can come alive — oh yes, it can.

Sure ... {laughter} ... Sounds great. ... It sounds more than great. It sounds wonderful, OK? "Oh, that it would be true. Oh, if it could be true for me."

These words at one time used to build resonance, strength, and power. Now you use them to ridicule and criticize yourself and to remind yourself that there is something wrong — still very wrong — with you. Words. Words that at one time brought possibility now, for far too many, bring only pain. And you get to a point where you feel: I don't want to hear about making peace and having overflowing magic and miracles. I don't want to hear about creative processes more exciting than the creation itself. I don't want to hear about tangles and briers and limitations. I don't want to hear about transcending and transforming.

And your life can be filled and overflowing with rewarding friendships and intimate relationships, with meaningful work and with fulfilling successes. You can discover the uniqueness of your own worth and your own value.

Because there's too much longing. There's too much ridicule and criticism, too much pain.

Yet you can't really walk away. You can't really turn away. The fault is not in the words. Perhaps it is in the limited meaning and the misunderstanding of the words, but it's not in the words. But the fault is not in you, either. No, the fault is not in you, either. The fault lies in the misconceptions and misunderstandings of what the Shadow is.

Special Note

In subsequent chapters of this book you will work directly with your Shadow, and you will need to have one of your Counselors with you when you do. You will also be working with your Higher Self.
If you are not familiar with your Counselors, we can suggest Lazaris' tape called **The Unseen Friends** *to introduce you to your male and female counselors, specialist counselors, and your inner child and adolescent.*
We can also suggest Lazaris' book **The Sacred Journey: You and Your Higher Self** *for learning to work with your Higher Self. If you need help finding a bookstore that has The Lazaris Material or wish to order directly from us, please call Concept: Synergy at 1-800/678-2356.*

Resources

The following Lazaris tapes are helpful in working with some of the issues in Chapter 2 or offer further exploration of related areas:

Healing the Child Within
Healing the Adolescent Within
The Unseen Friends
Utilizing Night Dreams To Create Greater Success

The following book and its optional taped meditations are a definitive process for coming in contact and learning to work with your Higher Self.

The Sacred Journey: You and Your Higher Self

2

What Is the Shadow?

But the Shadow is not only dark. There is also the Light Shadow who comes to you as the Monumental One, or as the Dream Weaver, or as the Protector. It comes not as Judge, but as the Compassionate One. It comes not as Betrayer, but as the Benefactor. And it can come to you not as the Denied Self, but as the Whole Self.

— Lazaris

The Shadow is made up of all the stuff that you have denied, that you discount, that you defend yourself against, that you distract yourself from — all the aspects of you that you pretend don't exist — or (if they do exist) are "no big deal." The Shadow is made up of all the stuff you learned to resist and that you refused to accept.

As a little kid you learned: You shouldn't be so selfish, you shouldn't be so greedy. You should do this, you shouldn't do that, you shouldn't do the other.

The Light Shadow, the Golden Shadow ... so pure, so filled with love and intimacy ...

You shouldn't question so much, you shouldn't, you shouldn't, you shouldn't.

And as a good little boy or a good little girl trying to become "idealized," trying to win favor, trying to survive ... {laughter} ... you did what you were told. And you shoved your selfishness and your greed and your self-centeredness behind you, pretending it did not exist. "In what hand? What are you talking about? Well, it doesn't matter." You discounted and you defended: "I am not, I am not, I am not."

But you didn't just stuff the dark stuff, the ugly stuff, the stuff that society says is bad and wrong and sinful and terrible and immoral and all that. You also denied the good stuff because of the messages that you got: Don't be so curious, don't be so inquisitive, don't be so honest, don't be so in touch with your feelings, don't be so creative, don't daydream like that, don't be that inventive, don't ask questions.

You also denied the good stuff because of the messages that you got: Don't be so curious, don't be so inquisitive, don't be so honest, don't be so in touch with your feelings ...

And you got all of those messages not just from mothers and fathers and siblings and extended family, but also from a society of television, a society of education, from a society of religion.

And all of these things — dark and light — got shoved behind you into what is called the Shadow. Your Shadow contains all the stuff that your adaptive child elbowed out of the way in its attempt to survive, in its attempt to find security, in its attempt to belong and to have some sense of self — called self-esteem. It is all that your panicked adolescent scattered in order to become idealized, in order not only to belong and to have a sense of self-esteem, but also to be accepted and to be approved of, to gain praise, if not from the family, then from peers.

All that the child elbowed out in its adaptiveness and all that the panicked adolescent scattered in its need for absolutes make up and become part of your Shadow.

And this you know, this you understand at least theoretically. What those parts are you sometimes have forgotten, but nonetheless you understand the concept.

Indeed, your Shadow is also made up of all your aggression. As little girls particularly, but also as boys, you weren't supposed to be aggressive at all or *that* aggressive, respectively. And you weren't supposed to be ambitious, because ambition is "bad and wrong." "You know what ambitious people are like." And so you believe you shouldn't have any of that.

All your weakness and lack of reliability, your lack of preparedness, was all shoved behind you, because it didn't conform with this "idealized self" that you were supposed to be to make them proud, to make them happy, to make them decide to let you live another day, another week, another month or year. All your insecurities were shoved away, denied, re-dressed as something else.

The Shadow is also made up of your lack of character and lack of morality, and also of your pride and of your hostility. Hostility is more than anger, more than hurt. Hostility is an anger that wants to hurt, often produced by an anger that did hurt. Your pride, your hostility and avarice — that hunger, that thirst, that greed that can never be sated — are also part of your Shadow.

It is also all that you have refused to be responsible for ... yet. It is so amazing, so ironic, so poignantly sad, that there are so many who become angry at the very idea that reality is a choice. They become very angry, some of them even violently angry, at the very idea that you have any choice at all. "No, it can't be. I refuse to accept it."

Yet when it comes to responsibility, they want to reserve the right to make choices. ... {laughter} ... "I'm not going to be responsible for that." Or, "I'll choose. I'll decide whether I will or will not be responsible for this." And it is so ironic that those who make a passion out of denying choice will demand it when it comes to responsibility. "There I do have choice, and I choose not to be responsible."

In fact, reality is filled with a myriad of choices. Almost everything is a choice. Almost. But among the millions of choices you make every minute of your life, responsibility is not one of them. You don't get to choose whether you're going to be responsible. You get to decide when, not if.

Everybody will take responsibility for their impact, for their creation. No matter how long they may deny it — no matter how long they may pretend — it is only a matter of when.

Some have learned to take responsibility quickly, with integrity, almost spontaneously. Others seem to deny and say, "No, I'm not going to be responsible. I'm not going to be responsible. I refuse to be responsible." But in time — it might be five years, ten years, twenty years, you will be. Perhaps it will manifest itself as some sort of illness, some sort of disease, and then you will be responsible.

The choice isn't whether you will be, but when you will be. And all the stuff that you want to postpone — all the stuff of responsibility that you want to delay saying, "I'll do it another day, another year, another decade" — all of that stuff goes into the Shadow. It never gets lost. There's no space. Where are you going to put it? Where are you going to throw it away? Only into yourself.

Maybe you hide it in your joints or in your organs — or maybe you hide it in the people around you in your reality. Perhaps you hide your hostility in your spouse or in your parents or in your boss. But eventually, you will come around to face it and be responsible. But until you do, it is contained within your Shadow.

Now these are the four components of the Shadow:

- what you have been taught and conditioned to deny,

- what the adaptive child elbowed away,

- what the panicked adolescent scattered,

- those aspects of yourself from your aggression to your avarice, and all that you will not be responsible for.

With most of academia, this is as far as it goes — this "black bag" or this "darkness" or this "ugliness" that you won't admit is you.

But, you see, your Shadow is more than that. And the truly frightening aspects of your Shadow are not the dark aspects. The truly frightening aspects are the light side of you.

The Light Shadow, the Golden Shadow (whatever color you call it) is made up of your power (that you

The Light Shadow contains the strength that embarrasses you and makes you frightened that you might be arrogant. It holds the fact of your true reliability that you fear might imprison you with duty and obligation.

pretend you don't have) and of your motivation, so beautiful, so pure, filled with the love and intimacy that seems corny, square, backward and stupid in your very fast-paced, high-tech world.

The Light Shadow contains the strength that embarrasses you and makes you frightened that you might be arrogant. It holds the fact of your true reliability that you fear might imprison you with duty and obligation.

And the Light Shadow contains all your true security — not in the stuff, but in the realness of self. It contains your true spiritual character — and personal character as well — that again is an embarrassment to so many in this very "hip" world of yours where being filled with character and morality is seen to be stupid, naïve, ignorant, backward, and square.

The Light Shadow also holds your real value and your worth — the love, the intimacy, and the caring you're capable of. And it contains your spirituality, which is, like avarice, a hunger and thirst not for things but for God/Goddess/All That Is. Avarice and spirituality, ironically, are very close to one another, the sides of a coin of thirst and hunger.

And the real depth and the real meaning of spirituality is also contained within your Shadow. Your Shadow contains all the true agendas that are often veiled by your surreptitious and hidden agendas. It holds your ability to be free of the past, to be, with dignity, self-determined. It contains your full capacity not just to be loved, but to love.

The Shadow contains your ability to have emotional dominion, to create a future, to be powerful, truly powerful — your ability to change reality not just for yourself, but also for those you care about and for the world that so relies upon you. All that which lies behind your hidden agendas is also part of your Shadow.

And finally, whether you're male or female, your Shadow contains all the feminine that you have denied in yourself: the imagination, the creativity, the wonder, the feelings, the perception, the conception that you deny in yourself.

And it contains all the masculine that as men and as women you have castrated, rendered impotent in yourself. It doesn't go away. It is there in the Shadow Self: all the feminine that you deny, and all the masculine that has been castrated.

That is what your Shadow is made up of. But it is important to understand: That is not your Shadow. That is what it is composed of.

The Shadow itself is more elusive. It is more elusive because it comes with many disguises. It wears many different masks. Within the consensus reality those masks and those disguises are often dark and frightening.

Many have seen the Shadow as the monster, the horrific giant monster, oozing with anger and pain and horror. Others of you have seen it as a Dream Stealer, the one that begins purposely to steal the dreams that need to be stolen, but then, out of hand, steals all your dreams and your creativity and imagination as well.

Others of you have seen it as the Objector — that part of you that, no matter what, objects to anything that you would do differently than you have done it before.

And the real depth and the real meaning of spirituality is also contained within your Shadow. Your Shadow holds your ability to be free of the past, to be, with dignity, self-determined. It contains your full capacity not just to be loved, but to love.

Many of you have seen it as the Judge that is a continuous, onward dialogue of judgments.

Others have seen it, perhaps, as the Betrayer. Maybe you've seen it as the unforgiving, unrelenting you. Or perhaps you have seen it as the Denied Self, the faces of Self that you have denied.

But the Shadow is not only dark. There is also the Light Shadow who comes to you as the Monumental One, or as the Dream Weaver, or as the Protector. It comes not as Judge, but as the Compassionate One. It comes not as Betrayer, but as Benefactor. And it can come to you not as the Denied Self, but as the Whole Self.

But even these various descriptions are but masks. These various descriptions are but disguises of the Shadow. The true Shadow Self is, for so many, still elusive. Many of you have known the faces and disguises of the Shadow. You've worked with its faces and disguises, but you have never worked with the Shadow itself. You have never come to face it without its mask, without its disguise.

And that is a result of the misunderstandings, of what is misunderstood of the Shadow, Dark and Light, and there are some very specific misunderstandings that you have.

Journal Pages

Resources

The following Lazaris tapes are helpful in working with some of the issues in Chapter 3 or offer further exploration of related areas:

Harmony: The Power Vortex
Balance: Releasing the Full Self
Negative Ego: Ending the Co-Dependency
The Crisis of Martyrhood
Harnessing the Power: Magically Ending Martyrhood
Freedom from Self-Pity
Freedom from the Unspeakable: Jealousy, Envy, Rage

3

Seven Truths about the Shadow
(Setting Straight Some Misunderstandings)

> *Your Shadow contains the Lost Depth of Soul. And it contains the Lost Depth of Spirit, of an imagination that imagines itself, of a creativity that creates itself. That's where that stuff is. The Shadow has it — not as ransom, but as a gift when you're willing to own it and make peace with it and accept it.*
>
> *— Lazaris*

1: The Shadow Is Born with You

The Shadow is born when you are. It is there from the moment of birth, and it's there to hold sacred and to protect all the "stuff" that you are unable to deal with, that you are unable to accept. It is there as a repository to hold what you cannot comprehend, what you cannot cope with, what you cannot deal with.

When you really make peace with your Shadow, your life can be filled to over-flowing with all kinds of magic.

For example, as an infant, there are levels of shame that you simply cannot cope with, you cannot deal with. If you were to attempt to, perhaps you'd die. And so the Shadow takes it, and holds it sacred, protects it.

Certain angers, certain hurts, certain fears, certain levels of hostility that as a child you felt but could not handle the Shadow holds for you. When in adolescence passions are born, a flood of energy that you can't begin to "grok," the Shadow comes forth to hold, to embrace, to collect what otherwise would be lost forever.

It is as though your arms are filled with bundles and packages — far too many to carry — and things fall out. And you can't even bend over to pick them up. You don't even realize they've fallen out. But your Shadow comes along behind you and meticulously picks up all this stuff that you've dropped.

It is as though your arms are filled with bundles and packages — far too many to carry — and things fall out. You don't even realize they've fallen out. But your Shadow comes along behind you and meticulously picks up all this stuff that you've dropped.

In a sense, your Shadow picks up your litter, and it picks up the valuable treasures as well. As a child, as an adolescent, even as a young adult, there are too many things to handle. But to lose those things would be truly devastating.

And so your Shadow is there to hold these things sacred and to protect them until you are ready — to hold sacred the physical, emotional, mental and etheric aspects of you that you can't deal with.

Then your Shadow very meticulously starts returning the litter that needs to be disposed of properly. But it also begins to return the treasures, the beautiful gifts, the beautiful, wonderful energies that as a child, as an adolescent, and as a young adult you couldn't deal with — even that as an adult you could not deal with yet at your level of maturity. It returns them. Whether you think you're ready or not, it returns them — often during the Shadow Time — that time after the Wounding*.

It also returns it during the midlife crisis. Sometimes the changes come so quickly and demand seems so steep that it interrupts your daily routine to force you to look at what the Shadow is bringing you.

And again in the late life crisis, when you are past your 50s and come to face yourself, your Shadow shows you what you thought you discarded, what you thought you got rid of but never did — because it's important to dispose of it — and important to do it properly. The means are all that matters in the disposal.

Your Shadow is not your enemy. It's not there to sabotage you, though it may appear as a Betrayer, a monster. It is not there to hurt you. It is there to help you, because it holds that which needs to be disposed of and that which needs to be accepted in order for you to become real, in order for you to become whole, in order for you to accomplish what you have come into this and every other lifetime to be and to become. It is not your enemy.

It is born with you to hold sacred and to protect all the stuff that you cannot deal with, that you cannot accept. It is not your enemy.

* For an explanation of the Wounding, one of the Seven Faces of the Soul, please refer to the Lazaris tape **Giving Voice to Your Soul.**

2: *The Shadow Is a Being*

Your Shadow is a being. It is not a space. It is a being, a being that sometimes appears in this or that or the other way, but it is a being.

It is an entity, a living force. No, it is not human as you would define it, with a head and shoulders and arms and a torso and legs — not a human being as you sense human beings in your image. But it is nonetheless a being. It is an entity. It is not a thing, and it is not a space, though it may seem to be, though analogies may describe it as such. Nonetheless, it is a being.

And it is not a complex, as many of a psychological background want to presume it is. It is not a complex. It is a living, breathing being that exists, that has always existed, if you will, as a part of you.

Your Shadow is not a monster — though it appears to some as a Dream Stealer or as an Objector in its dark masks and disguises. And it appears in its light masks and disguises as well. But it is nonetheless a being.

It is not just everything you have denied. It is a being that is *holding* all the stuff that you denied. It is not just what the child has elbowed out and what the adolescent has scattered. It is the being that *holds* all that has been elbowed out and scattered. It isn't your aggression. It isn't your ambition. It's the part that *holds* that energy for you until you're ready to face and deal with your aggression, with your negative ambitions, with your lack of reliability, etc.

The Shadow is the enemy of your negative ego. Your negative ego hates your Shadow, is terrified of your Shadow, and sees your Shadow as its natural enemy. For the Shadow can destroy or master the negative ego, and the negative ego knows it.

It keeps all that denied femininity that you have thrown away. It keeps all the castrated masculinity. A being that has these things is the Shadow. The being that wears these masks and disguises is the Shadow — which is a being that is complicated, not a complex.

3: *Your Shadow Is the Enemy of Your Negative Ego*

The Shadow is the enemy of your negative ego. Your negative ego hates your Shadow, is terrified of your Shadow, and sees your Shadow as its natural enemy. For the Shadow can destroy or master the negative ego, and the negative ego knows it.

It is the negative ego with its yammering that says: "Don't go looking any deeper. You've found your Shadow. That's all it is. Your Shadow's mean, cruel, got it? Cold, distant, cruel, oh, terrible, terrible, cold, distant, cruel. Phony, shallow. Got it? OK, run, get away. That's enough. You don't need to know any more. Now get out of here. You don't need to look any further. You're ugly, terrible, rotten, and disgusting. That's enough!" ... {laughter} ...

The negative ego is a proponent of the idealized self. The ego is the one who says, "Don't be real, be acceptable. Don't excel, be mediocre, fit in, be normal, don't make waves, don't do anything new or different, be accepted. Don't accept yourself, be accepted by others. Never accept yourself, only get other people to do that — by hook or crook, by whatever means you need. Be idealized. Be whatever other people want you to be. Be anything but yourself, anything but real. Call it real if you like, but be anything but real."

Your Shadow says, "This is what you have to face in order to be real." The Shadow is a proponent and ally of your real self, whereas the negative ego is the ally of an idealized (not real) self. Your Shadow and your negative ego are natural enemies.

Your negative ego has never once told you the truth. When you're about to make an absolute fool of yourself, it says, "Go ahead! Go ahead!"

Your negative ego says, "Conquer your Shadow." You cannot conquer your Shadow. Your ego says, "Destroy your Shadow." You cannot destroy it. Your ego says, "Battle your Shadow."

And you can never win. Whenever you battle your Shadow, you always lose. Whenever you try to conquer or to imprison your Shadow, you always lose. Your ego and your Shadow are enemies. And your Shadow is the one that is the ally of your Real Self. Your Shadow is an ally of your Real Self.

Your Shadow stands between you and the idealized you and the real you. It stands between. It is the Energy Between. You've heard that phrase before. Your Spirituality is about discovering the Energy Between. Yes, the Shadow is dark, and you must go into that Darkness, into the pit, into the Abyss. You must cross Chapel Perilous.

It is the Energy Between that allows you to transform, to bridge from the old form to the new form, to "trans" from one form to another through the Shadow self.

You never get there through your ego self. You never get to be real by traversing your ego. Traverse your Shadow and you become real. It stands between and holds all the "stuff" that you need in order to be real.

See, you need this stuff. You need to dispose of certain things to get real, to be real. And you need to accept certain things to get real, to be real. And the Shadow has all that stuff. It is the ally of your Real Self, and therefore, truly, your ally. And the negative ego is the enemy of your Real Self, the enemy of the Shadow, and therefore, your enemy.

4: Your Negative Ego Always Lies … *The Shadow Always Tells the Truth*

Think about that for a moment. Look back over the decades of your life, and you'll realize that your negative ego has never once told you the truth. When you're about to make an absolute fool of yourself, it says, "Go ahead! Go ahead!" … {laughter} … When you've just done something brilliant, it tells you, "You're in your ego. You're being arrogant. You're being self-centered. You're getting all puffed up. Who do you think you are? You're a nobody. You're a nothing. So you did something great once. You won't do it again." … "Hey, I've got a shortcut. If you just make 'em feel guilty, manipulate them, intimidate. That's the way you have to go. It'll get you there, I promise. Rich and famous. You'll get rich and famous." … {laughter} … "Don't do this honesty stuff. Takes too long."

You see, you have made alliances already. You just chose the wrong "you." You made an alliance with your negative ego when you didn't know any better. That's why you need to "bust" and master your negative ego. You need to shift alliances from ego to Shadow. The ego always lies. The Shadow always tells the truth.

5: Owning Is Not Imprisonment

Owning your Shadow is not imprisonment. It is not attempting to contain it. It is not attempting to put it behind you so that it never, ever happens again. Ownership involves harnessing, not containing.

It involves freeing it, not imprisoning it. It involves using and directing the energy that your Shadow holds for you — the energy of your anger, the energy of your hate, the energy of your control and manipulation, the energy of your cruelty, the energy of your phoniness, the energy of your hostility.

Ownership is vital and alive. It is embracing and bringing it closer, not pushing it further away, not burying it deeper than you've already buried it.

6: Making Peace with Your Shadow Brings It Closer

Making peace with your Shadow doesn't make it go away. It doesn't make it leave you alone. That's called denying it. That's called shoving it deeper down inside of you, and then it will, absolutely, come at you as "fate" or the "way of the world" or the "nature of humanity."

Peace makes your Shadow more conscious. "Then somebody else might see it." They already do. You're the last to know. ... {laughter} ... Making peace is finding out what your Shadow needs and what it has of yours. That doesn't make it go away. It doesn't happen that way, because it is a part of who you are. It is not a temporary aberration. Your Shadow is not a tempo-

rary twist and distortion. It is part of who you are.
That's a very difficult thing to accept, we understand.
But when you do, there is unbelievable freedom to
take that very energy and to use it productively, con-
structively, consciously.

Peace doesn't push your Shadow deeper. Peace
brings your Shadow closer. And that's why so many
people don't want to do it. That's frightening. That
scares them.

*When you shove
it deeper inside
of you, then you
create situa-
tions in your
world that come
at you like
Bosnia ...*

"You mean my hostility is going to be closer to the
surface?"

Yes!

"Well, what good is that?" ... {laughter} ...

Then you can handle it. When you shove it deeper inside of you, then you create situations in your
world that come at you like Bosnia and Armenia and
Somalia and The Sudan and South Africa and inner
cities everywhere — and in the people around you
that treat you with hostility you think is theirs when,
in fact, it's yours. If you would make it conscious,
knowing that you're capable of that hostility yourself
— "Oh, I'd hate to think!" — knowing that it's yours,
then you can handle it. Peace doesn't make it go
away. Peace brings it closer.

7: *Your Shadow Contains Your Lost Depth of Soul and Spirit*

Your Shadow contains the Lost Depth of Soul. And
it contains the Lost Depth of Spirit, of an imagination
that imagines itself, of a creativity that creates itself.
That's where that stuff is. The Shadow has it, not as

ransom, but as a gift when you're willing to own it and make peace with it and accept it. The Shadow is not your enemy. It's not your nemesis. It's not out to hurt you.

Maybe your ego and idealized self feel hurt, but your Shadow is not out to hurt *you*. It is not your enemy.

~

These are seven misunderstandings that many of you hold, and each of you holds one or another of them. In order to own your Shadow, you need to know what it comprises. It is also important to understand the truths about the Shadow, and to correct the misunderstandings. Then you have a fighting chance, then you have a legitimate opportunity, not just to dance with your Shadow, but to own it, and to make peace. ...

When you really make peace with your Shadow, your life, your reality, can be filled to overflowing with all kinds of magic, all kinds of miracles. And beyond the peace with your Shadow, you can begin to make peace with your Self. And then truly your life can be filled with all kinds of magic, all kinds of miracles, rich and ripe, dripping with magic and miracles. You can come to know your Spirit, and your relationship with God/Goddess/All That Is can be alive and vibrant with life and embracing love. And your spirituality can come alive — oh yes, it can. ...

Resources

The following Lazaris tapes are helpful in working with some of the issues in Chapter 4 or offer further exploration of related areas:

Ending Shame, Part I: Infancy
Ending Shame, Part II: Psychic Contracts of Pain
Ending Shame, Part III: Those Adolescent Years
Ending Shame, Part IV: Adult Shame
Breaking and Replacing the Dark Shield of Negativity
Our Secret Prison: Discover and Break the Dark Law
Releasing Negative Ego
The Secrets of Manifesting What You Want, Part I
The Secrets of Manifesting What You Want, Part II
Unlocking Your Unconscious

4

Owning the Shadow

When you can own the Shadow, then it doesn't have to happen "out there" in your world, in the stuff of your reality. You don't have to keep tripping over it, banging into it, being confronted by it. When you can own it and make peace — then it doesn't have to come at you. In fact, it won't come at you.

— Lazaris

Well, the Shadow can seem a bit overwhelming. ... {laughter} ... Hostility, martyrhood, self-pity. But you see, what gets denied — whether it is stuff that you were taught and conditioned to believe, or what you denied because you couldn't handle it — becomes part of the Shadow. All the stuff the adaptive child elbowed out of the way so as to be the idealized self, so as to survive — all the stuff that the adolescent, in its panic and need for order and stability, scattered in

All that beautiful stuff that you so long to have can be a reality for you.

order to be accepted — becomes part of the Shadow. All this energy of aggression and avarice, all that you won't be, or think you can pretend not to be, responsible for gets shoved down in you.

This being that wears the mask of all you have denied is really a living, breathing, conscious entity that exists within the vastness of you. The Shadow is not a complex, but rather is a being that is complicated.

And once it's shoved down, it has to come up at you — in the world, in the players around you, in the intimates of your life, in the stuff of your reality.

When you can own it, then it doesn't have to happen "out there" in your world, in the stuff of your reality. You don't have to keep tripping over it, banging into it, being confronted by it. When you can own it — and after the ownership, make peace — then it doesn't have to come at you. In fact, it won't come at you.

And it's the same with the beautiful Shadow, so often ignored in most explorations. All the power and spirituality, all the genuine agendas of destiny — all that masculine energy and feminine energy that is so incredibly and poignantly powerful and beautiful — does not have to seem outside of you, either. It doesn't have to be beyond your reach as you admire and envy those who seem to have what you miss, those that seem to have all that power, those that seem to have all that spirituality, all that strength and beauty and wonder.

"Why not me?" Because that, too, you deny in yourself. Regardless of the words you wrap yourself in, if you deny it in yourself, it has to come up at you in the world and in the people around you.

But when it can come through you, then you can create its becoming conscious. Then you are not just a witness, but a participant — not just a spectator, but a vital participant, a player. All that beautiful stuff that you so long to have, that somehow you know you already have, can be a reality for you.

So often you've said, "I know I'm powerful, but why doesn't my reality reflect it?" Because you're not owning it from your Shadow. You may long for it, desire it, wish to embrace it and grab onto it. "I have affirmations. I have positive statements and positive thoughts, but it's not mine." But to whatever extent it is there, it is not there with the depth or with the richness and ripeness there could be.

Yes, the awareness and the information seem at times cumbersome, at times overwhelming and depressing. But when you can own and then make peace with your Shadow — and have an alliance with your Shadow — there is such a beauty, such an incredible wonder that on this side of the Shadow seems impossible — words to long for, to beat yourself up with, to feel in pain with — but on the other side of the Shadow they seem not only reachable, but are already in your grasp.

So how do you own this Shadow? How do you own this Shadow?

1: *Working with Your Higher Self*

First of all, we suggest sitting with your Higher Self or with one of your Counselors or one of your Guides (or whichever of your Unseen Friends seems most appropriate).

Sit with your Higher Self and talk about the misunderstandings. Sit down and talk with your Higher

Self about this one that was born with you who holds sacred and protects and returns to you the litter as well as the treasures you have left behind. Talk to your Higher Self about this being that wears the mask of all you have denied, but which is really a living, breathing, conscious entity that exists within the vastness of you. The Shadow is not a complex, but rather is a being that is complicated. Talk about the truths:

- Understand that the Shadow is the enemy of the negative ego.

- Understand that the Shadow always tells the truth, and the negative ego always lies.

- Understand more clearly what ownership means, what peace means. And understand that this Shadow — that you've run from, that you've hidden from, that you've tried to deny — holds the lost depth of Soul and Spirit and the creativity and imagination so essential to your spirituality.

Sit with your Higher Self and talk about which of the misunderstandings are yours. Change the raw materials — the beliefs and attitudes, the thoughts and feelings, and the choices and decisions you make about your own Shadow. There are the seven we've suggested, and there may be others about which your Higher Self tells you.

Workbook Page

Begin with a meditation with your Higher Self (or other Positive Guidance) about your personal misunderstandings about the Shadow. On the next three pages, write out the feelings and thoughts you have from this meditation.

Workbook Page

Workbook Page

Workbook Page

Now do a second Higher
Self meditation to explore
your misunderstandings,
and write your thoughts
and feelings about it on
the next several pages.

Workbook Page

Workbook Page

Workbook Page

Now do one final Higher
Self meditation, writing
your thoughts and feelings
about your misunderstand-
ings about the Shadow on
the next several pages.

Workbook Page

Workbook Page

2: *The Reflections of the Shadow*

The second step is to look outside yourself. Look outside yourself at what we call the reflections of your Shadow.

Look to your family: mother, father, siblings. For some of you, there will be an extended family of grandparents, aunts, and uncles, depending on the size of your family. Look to your family. They are not your Shadow, but they are reflections of your Shadow.

Look to your body, your physical form. For that is a reflection of your Shadow: too tall, too short, too heavy, too thin, disfigured here, deformed there, malady here, malady there. Look to the body — not as an absolute, but as a clue. Look "out there" to the family and to the body for what it is trying to say to you.

Look to the players in your reality. A player is an acquaintance that you always encounter. It may be someone at work. It may be a boss. It may be someone that you see every morning on the elevator. It may be somebody that you run into every third day at the 7-11.

Players are not intimate friends. You don't feel a closeness, a tenderness, a vulnerability or a trust with them. They're just people you deal with on a very regular basis. But they're players, not just "extras." They are players in your play.

"That person ... I always see them. I don't even know who they are. I've never met them. We've never talked other than a nod here or there." That's a player.

"This person who sits next to me, or that works across the hall from me, or that I have to deal with in this or that department." Look to them.

Then look to the intimates, for often you will fall in love with your Shadow ... {laughter} ... or you'll give your Shadow to them. Maybe they weren't that way when you began, but now they are.

Sometimes those of you who are so afraid of your own aggression, so terrified to admit that you might have an aggressive bone in your body, will marry someone, or find yourself in an intimate relationship with someone, who expresses not only their aggression but your aggression as well.

And it's not just your darkness they may carry. Some of you, so afraid to admit your beauty, your power, the wonder of you, will marry or fall in love with someone powerful and beautiful and wonderful. And then you may find yourself insecure, afraid of losing them, or jealous of them.

Sometimes the person may not begin as a reflection of your Shadow, but through the intimacy, through the closeness and vulnerability of the relationship, they become the Shadow. They become the martyr that you pretend you're not. They become the angry person that you pretend you couldn't possibly be. They become cold and distant, reflecting the coolness, the coldness, the iciness that you, who pretend to be only warmth and soft, squudgy love ... {laughter} ... won't admit that you are.

These are reflections, you see? The family, the body, the players, and the intimates reflect the Shadow.

Then look to the intimates, for often you will fall in love with your Shadow ... {laughter} ... or you'll give your Shadow to them. Maybe they weren't that way when you began, but now they are.

Workbook Page

MOTHER

Write about the aspects of
your mother you feel are
reflections of your
Shadow.

Workbook Page

FATHER

Write about the aspects of your father you feel are reflections of your Shadow.

Workbook Page

Workbook Page

Write about how some aspects of your body may be a reflection of your Shadow.

Workbook Page

Workbook Page

INTIMATES

Write about the qualities of your intimates which you feel are a reflection of your Shadow.

Workbook Page

MISCELLANEOUS

Use this space to write about reflections of the Shadow that aren't mentioned above.

3: The Patterns

Thirdly, look to the patterns in your life ...

Look to the exaggerated emotion. Now we have spoken so very often, so frequently, of the importance of feeling with intensity. We're not talking about looking at the emotions you feel intensely. We're talking about looking to the exaggerated emotions you feel.

"This person makes me SO angry that I could just explode. I could just shred them. I absolutely could just SCREAM at the top of my voice. I can't stand what they do!! The way they wear their hair! ... {laughter} ... Look at the shoes they have on!! Every time I see those it makes me want to scream." ... {laughter}

That's not intensity. That's exaggerated emotion. ... {laughter} ...

"Those blankety-blank drivers!! ... They don't turn on their turn signals. They are so inconsiderate. I just wish I had a shotgun. I'd blow that head right off and teach 'em a lesson or two!" ... {laughter} ...

Sure, it's irritating. Sure, you might wish to gesticulate your anger, but you get home and you kick and you throw things because this idiot, 45 minutes ago, 10 miles ago, didn't turn on their turn signal.

Or there's someone in your life you hate in a way that's not just intense, but exaggeratedly angry or frightened or hurt, devastated this way or that. It's exaggerated beyond its form. Look to the exaggerated emotions that get repeated, that won't go away.

Look also to the repeated negative feedback that you get.

"Everybody tells me I'm so pushy. I just don't get it. I have never, ever, ever been pushy in my life." .... {laughter} ...

"I never tell anybody what to do. In fact, I refuse to tell people what to do. They're the ones who make the decisions. I insist upon it. I demand it. I would not have it any other way. I won't let it be any other way." ... {laughter} ...

"But people say I'm so pushy." ... {laughter} ... "Who needs them anyway." ... {laughter} ... "I'll find different friends, people who can appreciate me. ... Now they say I'm pushy." ... {laughter} ...

"Hey, if I know what's right for them, can I help it?" ... {laughter} ... "Is that my fault? When I see them making some terrible mistake, isn't it only loving for me to demand, to insist, to make sure they don't? ... " ... {laughter} ... "When their life is all screwed up from dawn 'til dusk, isn't it loving of me to step in there and fix it all? And they call me pushy!" ... {laughter} ...

Maybe, just maybe, they're not all crazy. ... {laughter} ... Maybe, just maybe, they didn't all get together before life and decide, "Let's tell them they're pushy ... hee-hee-hee." ... {laughter} ... Maybe it's not a conspiracy that while you were sleeping the world met ... {laughter} ... and agreed upon a lie. ... {laughter} ...

"I don't get it. They said I'm a martyr. Me? I don't have a martyred bone in my body. I don't know why people don't understand that. They say I'm a martyr and that I punish them. I don't know why. I had nothing to do with it, nothing at all."

Look to the repeated negative feedback, and also (more frightening) look to the positive feedback.

Some of you are so terrified that you don't let yourself get positive feedback. "No, no, no, no, no, don't say that. No, don't say that. Can we change the subject, please? .... 'Cause I'm so afraid I'll go into my ego (says your ego)."

Look to your patterns of exaggerated emotion, both dark and light — light as well. "Every time I see this, I cry. Every time I see that, my heart goes out." Look to the repeated feedback — negative and also positive.

Look to your compulsions and your obsessive behaviors. Compulsive and obsessive behaviors aren't necessarily bad, but they reflect or show a pattern of your Shadow.

Look to your secrets — not to tell them, but to understand them.

Look to the lies that you live, the secret life that you hold, if only in fantasy. Thus, look to your fantasies as well.

Look to the patterns of exaggerated emotion both dark and light — light as well. "Every time I see this, I cry. Every time I see that, my heart goes out." Look to the repeated feedback — negative and also positive.

Look to the kind of movies that you secretly like to go to. It's really sort of *déclassé* to admit that you like the blood-and-guts, beat-'em-up violence. But, you see, somebody out there must like it ... {laughter} ... Somebody must, because they're paying an awful lot of money to go see it and say, "Oh, how disgusting! Oh! You know, there were eighty-five people there. I counted them." ... {laughter} ...

Look to the books that you would put in a brown paper cover, not because they're sleazy sex novels, but because they're shallow romance novels or whatever.

Look to your fantasies, your secrets, your lies, your obsessions, your compulsions. All of these are part of a pattern of something you're trying to get, something you're trying to find, but don't think you should — and you think this is the only way you can come across it.

Look to the betrayals, the abandonments, the humiliations, the rejections — all these are part of the pattern.

Now you may not find a pattern of yours in each category, but as you look to the categories ... nothing here, nothing there, but aha! Over here.

Some of you don't have exaggerated emotional responses; others of you do. Some of you may not think you have compulsions or impulsive behavior, secrets, lies or fantasies. They're not bad to have — "Oh, I'd better stop that!" But if you do, look to them and learn from them, for they reflect a pattern, or they are part of a pattern.

So you look outside yourself to the patterns. ...

Workbook Page

Write about the exaggerated
emotions you have that are
considered negative.

EXAGGERATED EMOTIONS:
POSITIVE

Write about the exaggerated
emotions you have that are
considered positive.

Workbook Page

REPEATED FEEDBACK:
NEGATIVE

Write about the repeated feedback you get that you would
consider negative feedback.

Workbook Page

Write about the repeated feedback you get that you would
consider positive feedback.

Workbook Page

OTHER PATTERNS:

Write about any other patterns you have that manifest as compulsive or obsessive behavior, secrets, lies, or fantasies — or patterns of betrayal, abandonment, humiliation, or rejection.

Workbook Page

4: *The Projections*

Fourthly, you look outside yourself for the projections. Reflections, patterns, and projections are separate things.

Take someone you hate. "Oh, I don't hate anybody." ... {laughter} ... Big clue to your Shadow. OK ... take someone you dislike intensely. ... {laughter} ... Take someone you know, but if you're absolutely convinced there isn't anybody ... {laughter} ... there are enough world figures out there. At least you can hate Hitler or certain barbaric people. And if you absolutely don't hate anybody, then you know you've got a Shadow filled with hate.

Take someone you really dislike, that really gets under your skin, and sit down and list out — write it out, don't just do it mentally — all the things about them that you dislike. Not lengthy paragraphs, but just a word or two or a list.

"I just detest this person because they're so arrogant, so self-centered, so full of themselves. They're dishonest. They lie half the time, not maybe physical lies, but they lie to themselves, and they lie about themselves. And they're so pushy, and so controlling with that.

"Well, I don't want to list too many (says your ego). How about disliking them because they're too generous, they're too loving, they're too naïve, they're too spiritual?" That's your ego talking, and you know it. Be honest. No one else is going to read your list. Be honest with yourself.

What do you really dislike?

Now not every bit of it is your Shadow. ("Oh, whew!") ... {laughter} ... There are some things that you dislike that you genuinely dislike. "This person is an abusive person, and I hate the fact that they do that." Does that mean you're abusive? Not necessarily at all.

But you list out all the qualities that you can think of, the forty, fifty, 120 of them, whatever. ... {laughter} ... And then you go through that list to find which ones of them are informational. "Yeah, this bothers me about them. This I don't like about them. This I even hate about them."

You can bypass the informational reasons that you do not like them, because they are, after all, just informational. Which ones really affect you? When you even think of them you just seethe inside. You find that something tightens up inside. And out of that many there may be three or four such qualities that really just get you. You tremble when you think of them. "I don't even want to put them on paper. I just don't even want to see the words."

When you have an intense reaction to one of those many qualities, that's one you circle. If it really, really gets you, that's one you want to note. Not that you necessarily do it in the same way, but it is part of your Shadow.

And as you go about looking at that person you dislike, list the qualities, and then pick out ones that really get to you. You're only going to find three or four, maybe only one or two that really do something to you. Those are the ones you circle.

Likewise, you take this same person, and you look at: "Despite all of this, though I hate to admit it, I admire some things about them." Even though they're this wretched person with 45,000 things wrong with them, you've got to admit, they are one powerful this, or one capable this, or that, or the other. "I hate it, I hate it, I hate it, but it's true. I wouldn't want to let anybody know!" You don't have to ... {laughter} ... just yourself.

What are the positive qualities in this person you dislike? There may only be four or five. And among them, there are those that make you the angriest. Which quality really gets to you? "I *hate* to admit this. It just bugs me. It just tears me apart to say that they are ... the words are like poison in my mouth!" It's part of your Light Shadow. It's part of your Light Shadow.

Now you reverse it, taking someone you really love — that you really, really love. And you list all the reasons why. "Let me count the ways. ..." List all the reasons why. The silly ones, the stupid ones, the profound ones, the poignant ones. You list them all out. Don't worry about ordering and prioritizing. Just get them out.

And likewise, look through their qualities. "This is informational. That's wonderful. This is wonderful. ... This one makes me cry. This one makes me weep. This one touches me so deeply. This one ... I have to stop ... because it's such an intensity for me ... not that I envy it, but I'm in awe of this quality they have. It's so precious, so cherished that it catches my breath." Those are the ones you want to circle.

And likewise with this person you love, they have faults, they have flaws, qualities about them, not overriding ones, that you don't like.

If you are in love with someone and they have no flaws, you are not in love with a real person. Many of

When you're working with the projections, you gather those with intensity from one person you dislike and one person you like. Don't use a scattering of people — just one person you dislike, one person you love, and then work it through.

you women have been "madonna-ized" and put up on a pedestal ... "Oh, I don't have any chauvinism toward women ... I worship women." ... {laughter} ... Sounds like fun, doesn't it? "Oh, oh, somebody's going to worship me. Oooooooh, I love it. Kiss my ring." ... {laughter} ...

But you're not real to them. You're not real to them, and soon enough they'll find your clay feet and will accuse you of betraying them. Many of you women know this. Many of you men know this as well. If you are loving someone, and they don't have a single flaw, you don't know them. You don't know them. You are just projecting something, but not a real person.

Now we aren't saying they have to have as many problems as they do beauties. There may be only two or three things, but what are the qualities that you dislike? And likewise, circle the ones that have meaning, that jiggle you, that jangle you.

When you're working with the projections, you gather those with intensity from one person you dislike and one person you like. Don't use a scattering of people — just one person you dislike, one person you love, and then work it through. And those qualities you find will be the qualities that are part of your Shadow Dark and your Shadow Light.

You lay the backdrop. You look outside yourself to the reflections, you look outside yourself to the patterns, you look outside yourself to the projections.

Workbook Page

Workbook Page

ABOUT THE PERSON
YOU LIKE LEAST ...

Of all the qualities listed at
left, choose three or four that
really "jangle" you and write
about those — plus one positive quality you admire.

Workbook Page

ABOUT THE PERSON YOU LIKE BEST ...

List out all the qualities about this person that you like.

Workbook Page

ABOUT THE PERSON
YOU LIKE BEST...

Of all the qualities listed at
left, choose three or four that
really affect you deeply and
write about those — and one
quality you dislike.

71

Workbook Page

Use the next several pages
to write extemporaneously
about what you've learned
in this exploration of
your Shadow.

Workbook Page

Workbook Page

DARK SHADOW STATEMENT ...

Write a concise description of your DARK SHADOW.

Workbook Page

....

....

....

....

....

....

....

....

....

....

....

LIGHT SHADOW STATEMENT ...
Write a concise description of your LIGHT SHADOW.

....

....

....

....

....

....

....

....

....

....

....

....

....

5: *Bringing It All Inside*

The fifth step is that you bring it all inside and you see — through the reflections, patterns, and projections — the aspects, qualities, characteristics, and phenomena of your Shadow. You're not seeing the Shadow; you're seeing *phenomena* of your Shadow.

"My Shadow is these things. My Shadow is these qualities. My Shadow has these characteristics, these personality traits, these idiosyncratic behaviors and functions and activities."

You bring it into yourself, and you start owning these qualities. And when you hear the phrase *I would hate to think this is true of me,* know that's your ego. When you hear the phrase *Oh, it's so embarrassing!,* know that's your ego.

OK, your ego's embarrassed. Do you care? Does it really matter to you? The enemy is embarrassed. Well, let's stop looking. Let's stop digging. If that were the standard in your world ... {laughter} ...

And you own it: "Now maybe I don't have these qualities in the same way my projection did, but this is what I am. This is part of my Shadow." And in this fifth step you bring it into yourself and start owning it. You start admitting it. You don't have to broadcast it, but you own it and admit it in yourself.

SPECIAL NOTE

When you have read the meditation in the next chapter, you will have additional tools for working with parts 6 and 7. For now, do them your own way, using the imagery in the meditation to supplement these steps in all your subsequent cycles of Shadow Work.

6: *Chasing after Your Shadow*

In the sixth step, you chase after your Shadow. In meditation, in the inner world of your Safe Place and beyond — in the Underworld, following the Ribbon of Road — you go looking for your Shadow. You have to go after your Shadow.

It's not just enough to say, "OK, OK, my Shadow has hostility, my Shadow is cruel, my Shadow is filled with rage and hate." That's not hard to say, particularly after you've said it a million and one times.

Those are qualities of your Shadow, but that is not your Shadow. You need to go into meditation and chase after your Shadow.

You need to get beyond the safety — or into the Underworld, following that Ribbon of Road, perhaps even leaving it to wander across the wilderness in search of this Shadow. It is an assertive, aggressive search, and when you find the hostility, you go into it.

When you find the cruelty, that hatred, go into it. Beyond your logic and reason, beyond your intellect, go into it and face not the quality, but the being that *is* hostile, that *is* hateful, that *is* cold and cruel, or punishing, or self-centered and subtly controlling in this way or that.

You can make a list of terrible traits and say, "That's me." That's not owning your Shadow. It's not owning it until you can go into it, chase after it and find it, wrestle with it, unravel it, get dirty in it, let it cling to you, let it be a part of you.

Own it.

7: *Your Own Meditation*

Use the meditation format (in Chapter 5), or create your own. Create a meditative technique, create a ritual, a dance, as a way to connect with and find your Shadow. Always have your Higher Self, or your Positive Guidance, with you. We're going to suggest a sundial, a huge sundial twenty feet, thirty feet, maybe fifty feet around, not standing on a pedestal but embedded in the ground. In the center of the sundial there is a vertical object that casts a shadow upon the place on this sundial where you can go to meet, to see, to experience your Shadow.

If you find you have a place that works more effectively for you, that's fine. But create some sort of ritual, some sort of procedure, some sort of meditative approach where you can go to encounter, to engage, to deal with, to get to know that Shadow. That also is part of the ownership.

Then you are ready to make peace with your Shadow and to create an alliance with your Shadow that can catapult you forward.

Journal Pages

Journal Pages

Resources

The following Lazaris tapes are helpful in working with some of the issues in Chapter 5 or offer further exploration of related areas:

Working with Your Shadow: An Imperative on the Spiritual Path
Getting More Magic Out of Your Meditations
Enhancing Visualization

Lazaris tapes are available from Concept: Synergy, 1-800/678-2356, P. O. Box 691867, Orlando, FL 32869

5

Engaging the Shadow: The Shadow Meditation

The secret to successful meditation is visualization. The secret of visualization is to know: More important than seeing with your eyes is seeing with your heart.

— *Lazaris*

SPECIAL NOTE: This following meditation is transcribed from the tape *Working with Your Shadow: An Imperative on the Spiritual Path*. As it is given here, it has been edited very slightly for the written form.

Some of you may prefer to have Lazaris do this meditation with you, and if you do, the tape is available from Concept: Synergy at the address given at left. However, this meditation can be done completely effectively by you alone: Either you can read the meditation until you easily remember each of the elements, or you can make a recording in your own voice (but only for your own personal use as it is copyrighted material).

Before beginning, dim the lights, and find a comfortable position. ...

The Shadow Meditation

Let yourself close your eyes.

As your eyes close, there is a certain privacy in the dimness behind your lids.

In the privacy and the vulnerability it affords, let yourself relax, begin to relax. Just let yourself relax in the way that you have learned, in the way you have become accustomed to relaxing.

Use your own unique method for relaxing. In the darkness, let yourself relax. Let yourself let go.

Sense the armor of denial, of discounting — the armor of defense and of distraction — fall away. Maybe you unstrap it as though it were literally a suit of armor. Maybe you sense it evaporating.

Let it drop away as you relax, as you relax, as you let go. The resistances and the reluctances ... let them go. The refusals ... let them go. Let yourself become gentle and vulnerable. You are safe. Let yourself relax. Let go.

And as you are relaxing, count down from five to one, and with each descending number, just let yourself relax a little bit more, just a little bit more, so that at the count of one, you are totally relaxed, at ease. Relaxed. At ease.

Five ... letting go.

Four ... that's right.

Three ... a little more.

Two ...

One ... One ... One ...

And as you are totally relaxed, allow yourself to enter the Safe Place, your Safe Place — that special place in nature where you know you are safe, where you feel safe. And as you sense yourself there, let yourself open your mental eyes and open to the senses. Let them come, ever so gently, the sights and sounds and smells.

Oh, yes, it may seem as though you're conjuring them, making them up, just pretending. And that's OK. Go ahead. Imagine, if not with your eyes and ears and nose, then with your heart.

Feel the sights, the sounds, the smells, and let yourself touch — perhaps with tips of your fingers or with the gentle part of the palm of your hand, or with your body.

Feel the ground beneath your feet or behind your legs if you are sitting. Feel the grasses or the rock or the raw earth herself. And taste the subtlety that is called safety.

And into this place, allow the Guardian, the Guide, the one who can help you. Perhaps it is your Higher Self. Let this one who can guide you come. Imagine that they are with you now. Welcome them, and be welcomed. Let yourself be loved with a touch, with a look, with an embrace. And love.

And ask — so important that you ask — to find your Shadow. You have had many hints over the years, many clues. You have seen the monsters locked inside you — the Dream Stealers, the Objectors.

You have felt and heard the words of the Judge, the Betrayer — the unforgiving and unrelenting, crippled and denied parts of yourself. You have seen the face of your Shadow reflected. You've seen the patterns of its dance. You have projected.

Now say to your Guide, your Counselor, your Higher Self: "I want to find my Shadow. Beyond its masks, beyond its disguises, I want to find my Shadow. And I want to go into its depth, into the very pit, into the abyss. I want to be free. I want to be free. I'm tired. I want to be free."

They look at you deeply, and they understand. And by their countenance you know they know that you are ready. Perhaps it is their hand upon your forehead or atop your head. Perhaps it is with a gentle touch of their thumbs upon your eyelids, but they touch you.

And as they touch you, you sense a golden light — a shimmering golden light — as though descending from the heavens above and rising from the earth. It is a shimmer of golden light that begins to surround you like a cocoon or like an egg, a shimmer of golden light that is lifting and descending ... descending, descending, lifting until you are totally enveloped, surrounded, cocooned, cradled in this shimmering, golden light.

And with each subtle breath, you breathe in the light, filling your nostrils. It descends through your air passages into your lungs, filling them, overflowing. With every breath, the skin, thirsty and hungry, drinks and absorbs the light, filling you.

And the more you are filled, the more you are surrounded. As the breath pulls in, you pull in the light. As the breath exhales, the light spreads to the farthest reaches of you — to fingertips, to toes, through every cell.

And you are so absorbed by the light that you don't even hear your Counselor or Guide or Higher Self reaching to you with a hand to lift you and to guide you. But you feel their grip, gently encouraging you to come.

You feel as though you glow with golden light, as though you leave a trail of glimmers upon the land. And this one, who has come to guide you, takes you from this safe place ... out there, out there. For some-where, over those hills or through that thicket or beyond those mountains, there is a dial of the sun.

And so it is that they will guide you. So it is that the two of you will go searching not for Shadows, but for a sundial — a sundial huge and majestic, embed-ded in the ground.

Go as you will now, for what lies beyond safety is your own unique terrain. It may be familiar, as you may have travelled it so many times. Or it may be new, as you search for a sundial.

And as you make your way, this one who guides you will speak to you of what you misunderstand. It will speak to you, this one, of a Shadow that was born with you, that holds sacred and protects all that you could not deal with or accept — all the litter, all the refuse — and all the power.

Perhaps this one talks instead of a being who has characteristics, but is more than that — that is a living being. Perhaps it speaks of the Shadow as an enemy of ego, an ally of a Real Self — or of how an ego lies, while a Shadow tells the truth. Perhaps it talks of own-ership or of peace. Perhaps it speaks of a lost depth of Soul and Spirit.

Make your way, and listen ...

Make your way, leaving a trail of golden light. Make your way ...

And as the day passes into night, you travel together, leaving a trail of golden light.

Perhaps you are fighting the tangle of a thicket, climbing rocks, descending cliffs, following the shore, crossing the high plain ... looking for a sundial.

In the middle of the night, you think of your reflections: the family, the body, the players, the intimates. Maybe you think of the patterns, the exaggerated anger or fear or hurt, the exaggerated loneliness, despair, hopelessness, or shame.

Maybe you think of the feedback that others, no matter who they are, seem always to give you. Compulsions, impulses, secrets, lies, fantasies. Perhaps you think of the humiliations, the rejections that seem always to happen to you, the betrayals that seem to follow you and find you everywhere. Perhaps you think of the abandonments that by quirks and strange synchronicities always seem to happen.

Perhaps your mind focuses on one person you find so irritating, so unpleasant. Maybe your thoughts move to those you love, to the one that stands out. As you make your way ...

And before you know it, there you'll see it. Down there. Look, down there, off to the side. In the middle of the night, with the light only of the moon, you see a dial. Descend the hill, quickly now, and let yourself explore.

How big does it seem to be? What's it made of? Is it stone? Wood? Is it a metal? Is it clay that has been packed and baked in the sun? Is it inlaid mosaic, intricate? Just experience, even if it seems that you're just pretending.

As you stand upon the dial, making your way around — standing here, standing there — memories may come, images, people, your nemesis.

Move about ... just explore, just explore, just explore.

Your mother may be standing over there ... or your father ... or a particular sibling. That one you hate ... the nemesis you thought you had escaped ... that loved one. That person from work. Or a player. And amid it all there comes a sudden hush. And all of them disappear. ... Even the one who brought you here disappears until you are alone ... perhaps with just the moon, covered with clouds.

And yet in the blackness of the night, you see a silhouette, a form, a human form, cloaked, shadowed even in the darkness.

It is your Shadow. You feel a sudden chill. A sudden fright causes you to catch your breath. They move closer, they move stealthily, closer and closer. They are now very close, and you can hear them breathing in and out. You can smell a scent in the air that sends a chill through you. And you can see their hands — perhaps of a monster or a Dream Stealer or an Objector, perhaps gnarled, bony hands. And the hands lift not to you, but to their own hood, their own cloak, to reveal themselves.

You try to look away ... you try to look down, but you cannot. ... You lift your eyes to sense the Shadow. It holds everything you have denied about yourself, everything you've run away from, everything you pretended was not true ... everything ... See the Shadow.

However vivid, however vague, see the Shadow. Look at it. Sense it.

It is wearing a mask, that is true. It is in disguise.

Now you step closer and closer. Now you reach — tentatively, fearfully, but you reach: You reach for the mask, for the cloak — not to cast it away, but to remove it from the Shadow and place it where it belongs: the mask upon your face, the cloak upon your body.

And you sink into the depth, into the Shadow of your hostility, your hate, your bitterness, your fury, your rage, your aggression, your fear, your self-pity, your martyrhood, your sleazy "lowlifeness." Sink into the pit and feel. ...

And in the pit you wonder: How can you be this ugly, this wretched, this disgusting, and yet be loved? How could anybody love you? How could you be this vile and yet hope ever ...

Yet in this place, in the belly of your disgust, there is something else. There is someone else here who is just as lost and abandoned. It is your Shadow's Shadow, the Light Shadow, tender, vulnerable, fragile, pure.

The Light Shadow also lowers its hood, lifts its hanging head. Thinking it was lost forever, it sees you, and you see it. Let it reach out. Let it touch you. And you reach, and you touch. Let it lead you out of the darkness, out of this pit.

Take the ugliness, the bitterness, the venom and the poison of the Dark Shadow and use it as a force, a force to propel you out. And let this Light that now fills you compel you to pull you out. One to push you out, and the other to pull you.

And as you emerge from the darkness, this Light Shadow leans toward you, its mouth close to your ear. You can feel the warmth of its breath, its scent. And it whispers to you — perhaps just one word, perhaps a phrase. It will whisper in your ear. ...

It is the one who brought you here that awakens you to warmth, to the streams of light of the sunrise, to the morning light after the night ... And they embrace you, and they tell you how they love you.

In ways you do not yet understand, you have begun to know the Shadow — not to run from it, but to own it — to stop running, in fact, and accept it. And to use it: to use the darkness as a force to propel you, and the Light as a resonance to compel you.

They hold you. And you bury your head in their shoulder, their breast, their chest, in their love, knowing that you will follow the trail of golden light to find your way home. ...

And in a moment you will open your eyes. At the count of five, and not before ...

One ...

Two ...

Three ...

Four ...

And five ...

Let yourself open your eyes and exhale sharply. Let yourself return. ...

Journal Pages

Journal Pages

Resources

The following Lazaris tape is helpful in working with some of the issues in Chapter 6 and offers further exploration of the Higher Self:

The Gentle Walk: Step-by-Step Intimacy with Your Higher Self

6

Making Peace with Your Shadow: Dialoguing with Your Shadow

> *As you pass from "hour to hour" — section to sec-*
> *tion — 12 of them in all — you may hear voices,*
> *you may hear snippets of dialogue, old snippets of*
> *tapes run so long ago. ...*
> *— Lazaris*

Again, always have your Higher Self or Positive Guidance with you. Work with the sundial at your own tempo, at your own pace. Go back there to discover more of your own Shadow. Clear out your own misunderstandings, and look outside at the reflections in your reality, at the patterns of your reality, at the projections in your reality — bringing them inside, going after them, searching for them, going to that sundial.

Always have your Higher Self or Positive Guidance with you.

See it there, this huge disk, flat upon the ground. And as you stand upon it in the darkness of night — no, this sundial doesn't tell the time, but rather reveals the Shadow.

The Shadow will reveal those people in your reality who are holding pieces of your Shadow — the mother, father, sibling, or offender from your childhood or adolescence, standing here or there upon the dial. That person you know that you keep bumping into over and over again in your life that you had no idea was part of your Shadow ...

"What are you doing here?"

"I'm a part of your Shadow."

It may be an intimate in your life or one of the other players that seems obvious. They may show up there, standing at certain places as you move about from one hour to the next, from one place to the next. And when you see them you ask, "Who are you, and why are you here? What part of my Shadow do you hold? What role do you play?"

And they may answer: "I am your anger. I am your aggression. I am your hatred. I am your coldness and bitterness. I am your judgmentalness. I am your arrogance." All these ugly sides of self. All carry pieces of your Shadow that you take back, that you need to own.

As you pass from "hour to hour" — section to section — 12 of them in all — you may hear voices, you may hear snippets of dialogue, old snippets of tapes run so long ago. You may hear that voice saying, "You'll never amount to anything. You're just a dumb klutz. You can never do anything right. You never finish what you start. Here, let me do it. You are such an embarrassment. I wish I'd never had you."

Or you may hear the voice of that ex-spouse or ex-partner saying to you that thing that causes you to cringe, that is like fingers on the blackboard. Perhaps you'll see scenes, little snippets of your past as you wend your way along.

Once again, have your Higher Self or Positive Guidance present. There will be a hush as the Shadow comes — that being that holds all of this for you will come to reveal itself with its mask. This is where you can work with it, where you can go through the process not only of discovering and owning it, but also of making peace in an alliance with the Shadow.

Here in this very dial you can begin to own the Dark Shadow, for that is where you must begin. That's where you must begin, for the Light Shadow is much heavier, much more intense than the dark.

Therefore, you don't tackle the highest hurdle. You go after the lower ones first. You deal with the Dark Shadow first so that you can become ready to face the Light Shadow.

Upon this dial you can own the Dark Shadow, and here also will show up the Light Shadow — those people in your life that represent the Light Shadow, those phrases that you heard, that one teacher that was so important to you, or that one friend who made that comment, or the one beautiful incident that occurred that somehow haunts you, that beautiful something that you did that is reminiscent of or is a clue to your Light Shadow.

But the Dark Shadow comes first, and it comes in disguise.

Upon this dial you can own the Dark Shadow, and here also will show up the Light Shadow as well — those people in your life that represent the Light Shadow, those phrases that you heard, that one teacher that was so important to you, or that one friend who made that comment, or the one beautiful incident that occurred that somehow haunts you.

So how do you make peace with the Dark Shadow? How do you do that? How do you make peace? How do you create an alliance?

The Dialogue with the Shadow

Always have your Higher Self or Positive Guidance present ...

The first step we've talked about many times. You come to meet the Shadow, and you talk to it. "Hi there. What's your game? What's your number? What's going on? Who are you?" You dialogue back and forth. "Why are you here? What are you representing? What mask is that you wear? What costume? Talk to me. Object. Tell me what your point of view is. Express yourself. I'll express myself. We'll argue. We'll fight. We'll call each other names, but we'll dialogue it together."

And in the process of that dialogue, what you want to find out is what your Shadow needs from you to make peace — not to be your friend necessarily, but to make peace. What does your Shadow need from you to be at peace?

Now, you don't want to give it to the Shadow yet. You just want to find out what it needs. And you always want to have your Higher Self or a trusted Unseen Friend there to interpret, to give you the permission to believe what you're hearing.

"Well, I thought the Shadow always tells the truth." It does, but you don't always understand that truth. Your Higher Self does. Now that bristles some negative egos. But your Shadow is far too complex for you to understand it completely. However, your Higher Self does understand it.

If you ask, "What do you need from me? What do you need from me?" it may say, "I need your left eye."

You may think, "Well, of course they're speaking figuratively. They're talking about the way I view receiving, the way I view feminine energy, the way I view the world from that feminine side. I need to pluck out this eye and give it to them — figuratively, of course. So sure, I understand that. I'll give you my eye."

But the truth may be that one thing that might give them peace would be your left eye — literally. And if you go ahead and do that in meditation without asking permission, without checking with your Higher Self to see what they mean and whether it's all right, you may be in great jeopardy. It may so happen that you have an accident where you get your left eye poked out. And in the horror of that, in the process of that, you might do a lot of soul-searching and come to discover who you are. Alas! Your Shadow told the truth. When it took out your left eye, it was at peace.

"Whoa! I'm not sure I'm willing to do that." And we agree!

But if you check with your Higher Self, they'll tell you, "No, they mean it literally. Do not give them your left eye. Find out what else they need."

Suppose your Shadow says, "You've got to give me all your money."

You think, "Of course, they don't mean it literally. What use would they have for that? I see what it is. I have to give up physical possessions. OK, I've got that. I know what that means. I'm smart enough." And six months later you're bankrupt, losing everything, having nothing. Some people have come face to face with their Shadow and have made peace with it, and they're destitute in the debacle of their reality. "Gee, I didn't know they meant it literally." That's right. That's why you always check with your Higher Self.

You may not understand the depth, the intricacy, the complexity of the truth the Shadow tells, so you always check with them. "What do you need?" As you dialogue, always clear it with your Higher Self.

Then in reverse, you ask: "What do you have of mine? What do you have that belongs to me?" Not "what gift" in the sense of a wonderful treasure that they'd like to give you that's theirs. No. It's already yours. "What do you have that's mine?"

And again: Check it with your Higher Self. "Is that what they have?" They may say: "No. That's what they have, but you're not understanding it." They're telling you the truth, but you don't understand the depth of that truth. Ask further. Ask further.

And as you work with them, with your Higher Self interceding and interpreting, there will come a point when your negative ego will say, "Hey, you know enough. You don't need to talk to your Higher Self. Just go on your own."

Because, you see, your negative ego is the enemy of your Shadow and would love for you to screw up. Then it will say, "I told you so." And we'll tell you this: If you'll always remember this, you'll be safe, you'll be fine, but if you forget it, know that it's your negative ego. Know that it's your ego. If your Shadow says, "I need this," and you say, "OK," without checking it, know that you're in your ego. You might as well stop right there, get out of the meditation, and come back another time, because you're in your negative ego. "Oh, no, I just forgot." Not true. "No, no, no, these are the extenuating circumstances." Doesn't matter. You're in your ego. You're in your ego if you forget this little proviso, this little asterisk, to always get permission both in terms of what they need from you and in terms of what they have that is yours.

"Well, I didn't have time. ..." It's all negative ego.

The first step is to dialogue and to find out what it has of yours and what it needs from you — cleared by, interpreted by, understood by your Higher Self, who knows your Shadow in ways you can't begin yet to know it.

Now, you don't give what it needs yet. And you don't take what it has yet to make peace and form an alliance. There are a few more steps left.

Journal Pages

Journal Pages

Resources

*The following Lazaris tapes are helpful in working with some of the issues
in Chapter 7 or offer further exploration of related areas:*

A Cherished Secret of Success: Resonance
Crafting the Life You've Always Wanted
Making This Your Last Lifetime
The True Magic and Power of Waking Up and Staying Awake
Waking the Magician: Sacred Return to Oneness
Your Future Self

7

Creating the Alliance:
Regaining the Energy Between

And then you make peace. You give to your Dark
Shadow what it needs. And you take what has
always belonged to you. And you give to your
Light Shadow what it needs, and you take what
has always belonged to you.

— *Lazaris*

Taking the Mask of the Shadow

Now that you have dialogued with the Shadow, as
in the meditation you reach out to take the Mask of
the Shadow. Now it may be made of *papier-mâché*, or
it may be a mask made out of metal, wood, or whatever. And you take it — not to throw it away, but to
put it on. Remember always to have your Higher Self
or Positive Guidance present.

The Shadow is
not your enemy.
It holds sacred
what you need
to become whole
and to live your
Spirituality.

So here you are. You recognize that your Dark Shadow is filled with hostility. And here stands this personification: beady eyes that stare into you — if they were knives they would shred you. You would be bleeding to death. Hateful eyes filled with that bitter, tight, taut look. Maybe it's a monster that's heaving and sighing and oozing all kinds of poison and terrible infectious stuff — this hideous hostility that wants to hurt and twist and destroy. It spills and spews all over you, and you're covered with its gunk. But you find out what it needs from you and what it has of yours.

What does your hostility have? For one thing, an intensity of energy and a will like you've never seen — and a vision, in its own negative cast, like you have never known. Hostility has an intensity about it that is more immense than almost any other emotion.

Now you reach out and take the mask of hostility, and you put it on. You smell your hostility, you feel your hostility, and it's slimy and greasy and disgusting.

You put on the cloak of your own hostility, and it's wet and it's ugly and it's vile. And you wear your hostility and see through the eyes of your hostility. And you feel and feel and feel it. Just stay with it until you practically cannot stand it anymore. It is at that point that you move to the third step.

Entering the Abyss

Let yourself be dragged down into the pit, into the abyss, into the darkness where there are no words, into the pit of despair, of hollow emptiness, of a void.

Facing the Paradox

In the void you face the Paradox. The paradox may express itself as: "If I am this ugly, if I am this vile, how could I possibly be spiritual? How could I possibly be loved by my Higher Self, or by anybody, for that matter? If this is really true about me, then how could I possibly ever grow and be evolved?"

And indeed when you're dealing with the Light Shadow, there is a similar paradox: "If I'm this powerful and this incredible, why isn't my life reflecting that same power? If I am this beautiful and this phenomenal, why haven't I already finished my lifetimes?"

Now, in a consensus reality, the way that people handle paradoxes is to choose one thing or the other. One thing or the other, right? The either-or world in which you exist seeks singular authority: "Either I am this ugly, or I am that spiritual." Either/or, either/or, either/or.

And there are those who conclude: "I am this ugly, and therefore I am not spiritual at all. I might as well abandon my spirituality." And there have been those who have done so. Or they decide, "I am this spiritual. I don't care what anybody says. You're trying to make me see myself as something I'm not! My Higher Self is tricking me, betraying me. You're telling me that I have hostility when, in fact, I know I'm a spiritual person, and spiritual people don't have any hostility. And it infuriates me no end!" ... {laughter} ...

You see, you tend to try to resolve paradoxes by either/or. It's this or it's that. Just pick one. That's called mediocrity, and it's not so. You sit with paradox. "I am this vile and this loved. Both are true."

And then you will be led out of the darkness by your Light Shadow — by the power, motivation, reliability, security, beauty, wonder, true feminine energy, and true masculine energy of your Light Shadow.

"But I don't understand that."

It's OK that you don't. You don't have to understand it. You just have to let it in: "I'm this awful and I am this beautiful. I am this ugly, and I am this beautiful. I am this vile, I am this spiritual. I am both of these."

And you sit with it. Patience: paying attention. You listen, because out of the paradox will emerge not one or the other, but something that's in between, something that is common both to your vileness and your spirituality, both to your ugliness and to your beauty. It's not a compromise — a little bit vile and a little bit beautiful. ... {laughter} ...

No, it's something that you always are, whether you're being vile or whether you're being beautiful. That's the Energy Between. And as you sit with the paradox, waiting, watching, listening, feeling, you will discover that which is common to both of these contradictory, paradoxical positions.

And then you will be led out of the darkness by your Light Shadow — by the power, motivation, reliability, security, beauty, wonder, true feminine energy, and true masculine energy of your Light Shadow. You will be led out of the darkness by the depth of your Soul that you've lost, by your Spirit. You don't leave the darkness; you are led out of the darkness by your Light Shadow, which you likewise dialogue with.

You learn what it needs to be at peace, and what it has of yours, with the help of your Higher Self.

And then, you make peace. You give to your Dark Shadow what it needs. And you take what has always belonged to you. And you give to your Light Shadow what it needs, and you take what has always belonged to you.

Then you can use all that darkness, with its intensity, to propel, to change, to transform, and you let all the resonance of the Light pull you, change you, pull you into the new.

The Dark becomes a force; the Light becomes a resonance. The force pushes, the resonance pulls. The force propels, the resonance compels.

As you recognize your hostility and the immensity of energy, the immensity of caring, that lies at the root of hostility, you can discover the beauty of your passion and compassion, using the force of your own hostility to propel you out of the illusion you've been in. At the same time, the passion and compassion pull you into the new reality. You are pushed and pulled simultaneously, catapulted into a new reality.

And that's how you make your alliance. It's not a friendship. You don't love the fact that you have hostility. But you can be allies and work together. You can be at peace with one another. "How can I be this hostile and this loving?" What's common to both? Caring, for example, is common to both.

How can I be this much of a martyr, yet this able to create and to be spiritual? What's common to both? Transformation, transformation. Martyrs — not to be proud of it — have a phenomenal capacity of transformation. The Victim whines and complains because their reality is full of clouds and rainy days. "Everybody rains on my parade. Nothing ever works for me." The Victim doesn't have the power to make it rain, but they can imagine and pretend even when it's not there.

Martyrs are so powerful that they literally make it rain. You really do get overworked. You really do get unappreciated. You really do get misunderstood. It's not enough for you to pretend. You have to create the concrete reality and then spend your life trying to prove to everybody: "See how wet I am?" ... {laughter} ... Whereas the Victim imagines everybody's raining on their parade, the Martyr makes the rain fall! ... {laughter} ...

Now that is a power of manifestation extraordinaire. Martyrs can find people in a crowd that will take advantage of them. You have a sense that is phenomenal! ... {laughter} ... The meaning and energy of that which you use to martyr yourself is something you can use to propel yourself never to be a martyr again.

You can use all that energy to be something else — a transformer of reality. And you can use the resonance — the Light Shadow — to pull you into the New Reality. And this push and pull catapults you, produces miraculous change, produces magical change. And you will knock yourself over when you do it. "Oh, my God, it works."

But it involves, you see, clearing out the misunderstandings so it's not "the enemy". It involves owning what it really is. It involves talking with it, dialoguing with it, wearing its masks, sinking into the pit, and facing the paradox. Then you will be led out of the pit by the Light Shadow. Then, accepting both the Dark and the Light as true, one force propels you as the resonance compels you.

And then let the change occur.

And that is the Shadow Work that is imperative upon the Spiritual Path.

It sounds like a lot. And you know what? It is. But then, you see, you give yourself a lifetime. Shadow Work is the work that never ends. You will always be working with your Shadow. It is not your enemy. It holds sacred and protects what you need to become whole and to live your Spirituality.

With love and peace ...

LAZARIS

Journal Pages

Journal Pages

Appendix

Lazaris Seminars & Tapes
Books & Music
Calendars & Journals

Lazaris Seminars

In the years since 1974, when Lazaris began channeling through Jach Pursel, his only channel, he has created an ever-expanding number of avenues for metaphysical and spiritual growth. Among them are the delightful Lazaris Seminars.

Lazaris conducts seminars frequently in San Francisco, Los Angeles, Atlanta, Orlando, Newark, NJ, and occasionally in other cities as the schedule allows.

Ranging from Evenings with Lazaris to One-Days, Weekends, and three- and four-day Intensives, Lazaris seminars provide wonderful in-depth explorations of everything from clearing personal blockages to exciting emerging metaphysical and spiritual opportunities.

www.Lazaris.com

Please also join us in The Jach & Lazaris Room on the World Wide Web at **www.Lazaris.com**. This thriving website is home to more than 60,000 messages from the vast community of people worldwide who are working with The Lazaris Material. There is both a public area with invaluable information on The Lazaris Material and a private forum that contains Lazaris transcripts and messages directly from Lazaris to forum members. There are also fabulous messages and conferences, some of which include meditations done directly by Lazaris. To join, please contact the Concept: Synergy office at 1-800/678-2356 (407/876-4973 from overseas). We look forward to seeing you there.

Lazaris' Mailing List

Concept: Synergy organizes the seminars and publishes the Lazaris tapes and books. If you would like to be on our mailing list and receive information about Lazaris seminars and notification of new books and tapes, please call us at 1-800/678-2356.

Personal Growth Tapes

Tapes from the Evenings with Lazaris, three hours of discussion, tools and techniques, and a guided meditation.

1996: The Year of Wonder
Abundance & Prosperity: The Skill
Accelerating the Pace of Manifesting Success
Accessing the Incredible Force of Love
Activating Miraculous Success
Alleviating Your Life Lesson & Letting It Serve You
Backdrop of Success/Creating the New Fabric
Balance: Releasing the Full Self
Being Loved
Beyond Struggle: The Magic of Being Good Enough
Busting & Building Image
Busting Free: Beyond the Need To Control
Coming Home
Consciously Creating Success
Crafting the Life You've Always Wanted
Creating & Cultivating Your Spiritual Family
Creating a Brilliant Future
Creating, Building & Keeping Intimate Relationships
Crisis of Martyrhood
Crystals: The Power & Use
Developing Self-Confidence
Discovering the Adult
Discovering Your Subconscious
Dominion at Work: Engaging the Elements
The Elegance of Abundance
Ending Guilt
Ending Loneliness
Ending the Pain
Ending Self-Punishment
Ending Self-Sabotage
Ending Shame, Part I: Infancy
Ending Shame, Part II: Psychic Contracts of Pain
Ending Shame, Part III: Those Adolescent Years
Ending Shame, Part IV: Adult Shame
Ending Your Addiction to the Past

Continued on next page ...

Personal Growth Tapes ...

Escaping the Entrapment of "Perfection"
Escaping the Suffocating Web of Anxiety
Expanding Success Exponentially
Explore the Wonder: Intimacy/Love
Finally Accepting Self: Being Fully Loved
Freedom from Self-Pity
Freedom from the Unspeakable: Jealousy, Envy, Rage
The Gentle Walk: Intimacy with Your Higher Self
Giving Voice to Your Soul
Harmony: The Power Vortex
Harnessing the Power: Magically Ending Martyrhood
Healing: The Nature of Health, I
Healing: The Nature of Health, II
Healing the Scars of the Past, Charting the Future
I Deserve!
Incredible Force of Forgiveness
Inner Peace
In Search of Miracles
Intimacy
Intuition
Living Magically Every Day
The Lost Treasures of Joy
The Magic of Joy
The Magic of Receiving: A New Dimension of Success
Making This Your Last Lifetime
Mysterious Power of Chakras
The Mystery & Magic of Co-Creation
Negative Ego: Ending the Co-Dependency
New Dynamics of Processing & Programming
New Maps to More Elegant Futures
Our Secret Prison: Discover/Break the Dark Law
Personal Depth: Health, Wealth & Success
Power of Dominion
The Powerful Secret of Reflection
Programming What You Want
Prosperity & Abundance in the 1990s
Reality Creation: The Basics
Reclaiming Lost Depth of Soul: Awakening Your Spirit
Relationships That Work: Creating the Next Level
Secrets of Success in the Remaining Years of the Millennium
Secrets To Changing Anything in Your Life — Instantly

Self-Esteem
Self Worth / Self-Respect
The Sirius Connection: What It Can Mean in Your Daily Life
      (no meditation)
Standing on the Verge:
      Elegant Visions Creating Magical Successes
Stop Feeling Not Good Enough
Transforming Negativity: Enemies into Allies
Transforming Personal Fear into Amazing Success
Transforming Self-Sabotage into Lasting Success
The True Magic of Waking Up & Staying Awake
The Unseen Friends
Turning Potential into Successful Achievement
Utilize the Unknown Powers of the Magical Child
Utilizing Night Dreams To Create Greater Success
Utilizing the Incredible Mystery & Magic of Expectation
Utilizing the Power of Choice To Generate Profound Change
Waking the Magician: Sacred Return to Oneness
Winning the Manifestation Game
Winning: New Tools To Get What You Really Want
Working with Your Shadow: An Imperative on the Spiritual Path
Your Future Self

The Red Label Series

Meditation tapes to re-pattern your subconscious to allow more beneficial realities in specific areas.

Handling Depression/Loneliness
Happiness/Peace
High Energy/Enthusiasm
Improved Health/Balance/Harmony
Integrity/Honesty
Monetary Success/Personal Success
Personal Power/Power & Dominion
Productivity/Impeccability
Reduced Sleep/Improved Sleep
Reducing Fear/Worry/Stress
Self-Confidence/Self-Awareness
Self-Love/Love

Continued on next page …

Lazaris Videos

Full-color videos in VHS and PAL, two hours, all with meditations. Audio versions of all the videos are also available.

Achieving Intimacy & Loving Relationships
Awakening the Love
Developing a Relationship with Your Higher Self
Developing Self-Confidence
Forgiving Yourself
The Future: How To Create It
Listening to the Whispers
The Mysteries of Empowerment
Overcoming Fear of Success
Personal Excellence
Personal Power & Beyond
Releasing Negative Ego
Secrets of Manifesting What You Want, Part I
Secrets of Manifesting What You Want, Part II
Spiritual Mastery: The Journey Begins
Unconditional Love
Unlocking the Power of Changing Your Life

Lazaris Discussions

AIDS: A Compassionate Exploration
Healing Hurt / The Keys of Happiness
Lazaris Talks about AIDS with Louise L. Hay's Group
On Releasing Anger / On Releasing Self-Pity
On Releasing Guilt / On Receiving Love
Lazaris Talks with Vietnam Veterans
The Synergy of Trust
Beyond the Threshold / Editing the Film
Cleaning Chakras / Pituitary-Pineal Meditation
The Goddess Series, Part I
The Goddess Series, Part II
Handling Menstruation

Lazaris Blank Journals

Quotes by Lazaris, covers by Gilbert Williams. Two cover choices:

"Gathering Place" Cover
"Mist Angel" Cover

Lazaris Books

Please see the title page for books in other languages.

Lazaris Interviews: Book II
The Sacred Journey: You and Your Higher Self ...
Working with Your Shadow: An Imperative on the Spiritual Path

Lazaris & Peny Tapes

Discussions on a myriad of fascinating subjects from the delightful Evenings with Lazaris and Peny, plus one tape made "at home."

Feb. '92 Palm Beach Evening
April '91 Palm Beach Evening
April '86 Evening
July '86 Evening
November '86 Evening
SF March '87 Evening
LA March '87 Evening
At Home with Lazaris & Peny

Letting More Love into Your Life

Techniques and meditations from Weekends, Intensives, and One-Days

The Pillar of Light Meditation
The Depth of Chakra Meditation
The Tree of Love Meditation
The Circle of Love Meditation
The Circle of Forgiveness Meditation
The Reconnecting with Emotional Depth Meditation
The Igniting the Essence Meditation
The Double-Tetrahedron Technique and Meditation
The Tonal Creation and Manifestation Technique
The Radiance of Resonance Meditation
Weeding Negative Futures and Seeding Positive Futures
Creating Optimal Futures

Calendar

Quotes by Lazaris, art work by Gilbert Williams.

The Lazaris-Gilbert Williams Calendar (published annually)

Continued on next page ...

Connecting with Lazaris Tapes

A special series of 30-minute tapes, many with 28-day processes, for awakening, building dreams, and deepening a connection with Lazaris.

Accepting the Gifts of the Metaphysician
Allowing the Fun
Awakening Your Brain
Building & Achieving Destiny
Building Your Personal Dream, Part I
Building Your Personal Dream, Part II
Choosing Your Own Lessons
A Cherished Secret of Success: Resonance
Embracing Power
Empowering Your Imagination
Enhancing Visualization
Feeling More of Lazaris' Love: Blending
Getting More Magic Out of Your Meditations
Healing the Child Within
Healing the Adolescent Within
Hearing the Music ... Allowing the Magic
Letting Yourself Be Loved: Allowing Lazaris' Love
Loving Better, Loving More Deeply
Loving Someone More
The Magic of Solitude
Mind Meld: Higher Self
The Power & Beauty of Self-Acceptance
Receiving Clearer, More Helpful Answers in Meditation
Receiving the Healing from Your Higher Self
Renewing Chakras
Sharpening Tools: Awakening Desires

Tapes for Children & Teenagers

Lazaris with Beky Carter.

Relaxation and Self-Love/Good Health and Chakras (Age 4-10)
Expressing Emotions/Communicating with Parents (Age 4-10)
Expressing Emotions/Communicating with Parents (Age 11+)
Self-Forgiveness/Self-Love (Age 11+)

The Accelerated Journey Series

One-hour discussions with meditations, to accelerate your Spiritual Journey Home.

Breaking & Replacing the Dark Shield of Negativity
Building the Dream Your Higher Self Has for You
Chakra Link: You and Your Higher Self
The Crisis Tape
Discovering Your Personal Strengths and Unique Powers
Discover the Dreamer from Lemuria
Embracing Your Higher Self: Receiving the Love
The Evening Tape
Finding Your Bottom Line
Finding Your Own Peace
Freedom from Karma
Freedom from the Past
The Goddess: Beginning to Receive Her
High Magic: The Ritual of Receiving
Initiations of Magic
Longevity: The Healing Technique
The Magic of Our Spiritual Ancestry
The Mists of Manifestation
A More Powerful Causal Plane
The Morning Tape
Opening the Magic Door
Preparing for Achievement
Releasing Your Dreams & Visions into the World
Stop Negativity in Its Tracks
Unlocking Your Unconscious
Utilizing Solstice & Equinox Energy

Music Tapes ... Cassettes

Music written especially for Lazaris and featured in many of the Lazaris meditations on tape.

Prelude to Lazaris
Lazaris: A Spark of Love
Lazaris Remembers Lemuria *(also available as a CD)*
Lazaris & the Dolphins
Journey with Lazaris
The Love of Lazaris
Through the Vortex with Lazaris

Newest Tape Releases

Tapes from the Evenings with Lazaris, three hours of discussion, tools and techniques, and a guided meditation.

Activating & Utilizing Our True Core of Power: Love & Will
Becoming a Winner at Living Life
Crystals: Tools to Co-Creation
Developing & Utilizing Our Temporal Lobes
Enchanted Wisdom: Windows to the New World
Generating Abundance as Never Before
The Great Awakening
Lucid Dreaming: The Night's Labyrinth Revealed
Mystical Other: Beyond the Conscious Mind
New Horizons of Potential & Opportunity
New Strategies To Optimize Success
New Ways of Harnessing & Transmuting Negative Ego
Passions Awaken: The Soul's Call to Adventure
Rekindling the Thrill: The Magic of Enthusiasm
Secrets of Empowerment: Loving Beyond Self
Utilizing the Beautiful Unknown: The Empowered Path